*WHAT I MEANT TO SAY WAS

Well known quotes
Revised for the humor endowed reader

by

Laurie James

Have a Laugh on me

Laurie James

Your loving sister

ISBN: 1-4033-6251-3 (e-book)
ISBN: 1-4033-6252-1 (Paperback)

This book is printed on acid free paper.

1stBooks - rev. 10/15/02

TESTIMONIALS

Once I picked this book up I could not put it down. It may have had something to do with the fact that I was eating a peanut butter and jelly sandwich at the time.

Benjamin Franklin

Although not understood in Russia, the humor of Laurie James might be understood by you. In any case, she is a personal friend of mine and I like her, even though I don't understand a thing she says.

Nikki Tolstoi

I was extremely happy to have received a gift copy of Laurie's book. Some day I may even read it.

Winston Churchill

If I were alive today I would probably read this book.

Ogden Nash

Laurie James has a natural, inherited wit. We Germans (and she's one of us) have a long history of unbridled humor. Sie ist cuckoo!

Konrad Adenauer

CONTENTS

FORWARD

Many wise men have said many wise and memorable things. And, to be politically correct, a lot of women have said some darned brilliant things too. I wonder if any of them ever considered their comments might one day become historical quotes, printed in books of quotations, and repeated over and over by the rest of us.

If they did, would any of them have changed their minds and said, "Just a minute, what I meant to say was...."

I know I would.

Because most of those wise people are dead, and the rest may not be too sure of their status, I've taken the liberty of doing a little editing on their behalf. In this book you'll find below each well-known quote, a revised statement – one they might have said had they been given a second chance.

Once you've read them I'm certain you'll be saying, "Now why didn't they think of that in the first place."

I know I did!

Truth & Consequences

"Fish and visitors stink in three days."

Benjamin Franklin, 1706-90
American Statesman

* Mom, put that suitcase down, I didn't mean

you.

~~~~~

"Nothing in life is so exhilarating as to be shot

at without result."

Winston Churchill, 1874-1965
British Prime Minister

* I swear, she told me she wasn't married!

~~~~~

"Ladies, just a little more virginity, if you

don't mind."

Alexander Woollcott, 1887-
1943
American Writer

* I hadn't planned on visiting the Mustang

Ranch, but seeing as we're so close .....

~~~~~

"I did not have sexual relations with that

woman."

Wm. J. Clinton, 1946 –
American President

* I don't know, which one were you pointing

at?

~~~~~~

"I am as strong as a bull moose."

Theodore Roosevelt, 1858-1919
American President

* Underarm deodorant is useless when you're

wrestling grizzlies.

~~~~~

"There are only two classes of pedestrians in

these days of reckless motor traffic – the quick

and the dead."

Lord Dewar, 1864-1930
British Industrialist

* If you spotted the cell phone drivers before

they hit you – you're in the quick category.

~~~~~~

"Pigeons in the grass, alas."

Gertrude Stein, 1874-1946
American Writer

* Will the dry cleaning remove the brown

stains as well?

~~~~~~

"'Tis strange what a man may do and a

woman yet think him an angel."

Wm. Makepeace Thackery,
1811-63
English Novelist

* Can you believe that guy, what was his name

-- Buttafuoco?

~~~~~

"If I were not Alexander, I would be

Diogenes."

Alexander The Great, 356-323
B.C.
Conqueror

* Frankly, I'm just happy Mom didn't name

me Todd, or Lance, or Clive, or Nigel.

~~~~~

Laurie James

"I want to be alone."

Greta Garbo, 1905-90
Actress

* Can't I sit in the john for five minutes

without you barging in?"

~~~~~~

"If some countries have too much history, we

have too much geography."

Wm. Lyon Mackenzie
King, 1874-1950
Canadian Prime Minister

* Where the hell is Flin Flon, Manitoba?

~~~~~

"Well, if I called the wrong number, why did

you answer the phone?"

James Thurber, 1894-1961
American Humorist

* Da!

~~~~~

"Grass is the handkerchief of the Lord."

Walt Whitman, 1819-92
American Poet, Writer

* Never mind that, get this guy a Kleenex.

~~~~~

"The difference between genius and stupidity

is that genius has its limits."

Anonymous

* I'm not penning my real name to that one.

~~~~~

"We know what happens to people who stay

in the middle of the road. They get run down."

Anuerin Bevan, 1897-1960
British Politician

* Old men in hats, and blue haired ladies

driving a dead man's car - is there any way we

can get them off the road?

~~~~~

<u>Cosmetically Speaking</u>

"I have nothing to offer but blood, toil, tears

and sweat."

Winston Churchill, 1874-1965
British Prime Minister

* Sorry, I didn't have time to wash up before I

came to bed.

~~~~~

"There is no excellent beauty that hath not

some strangeness in the proportion."

Francis Bacon, 1561-1626
English Writer

* What's the deal with that Marilyn Manson?

~~~~~

"It is totally impossible to be well dressed in

cheap shoes."

Hardy Amies, 1909-??
English Couturier

* They might be expensive, but those

Birkenstocks are still ugly.

~~~~~

"When grace is joined with wrinkles, it is

adorable. There is an unspeakable dawn in

happy old age."

Victor Hugo, 1802-85
French Novelist

* Should grace be lacking, a little bit of plastic

surgery couldn't hurt.

~~~~~

"His face was of that insipidly pleasing kind

which women call "not bad looking.""

> Count Nikolay Tolstoi, 1828-
> 1910
> Russian Novelist

* Yeah, but wait 'til they see his hairy back!

He's a first cousin to Cro-Magnon.

~~~~~

"We don't bother much about dress and

manners in England, because as a nation we

don't dress well and we've no manners."

George Bernard Shaw, 1856-
1950
English Novelist

* Those of you with "HRH" in front of your

names – please report to **Etiquette Class.**

~~~~~

"Lycurgus used to say that long hair made good looking men more beautiful, and ill-looking men more terrible."

Plutarch, c.46-120 A.D.
Greek Philosopher

* Personally, I don't care what he said, I still say men in pony-tails look stupid.

~~~~~

"Anything one man can imagine, other men

can make real."

Jules Verne, 1828-1905
French Novelist

* That surgeon of Michael Jackson's – what a

genius!

~~~~~

<u>Politicians and Strange Bedfellows</u>

"Distrust all in whom the impulse to punish is

powerful."

Friedrich W. Nietzsche,
1844-1900
German Philosopher

* I warned you to stay out of Texas. Those

cowboys will lasso you to a chair quicker than

you can say "barbecue."

~~~~~~

"I have not hesitated to travel from court to court like a wandering minstrel. But always with the same song, or same set of songs."

Winston Churchill, 1874-1965
British Prime Minister

- I'm no different than any other politician, I can't help repeating myself over and over, and over, and over.

~~~~~

"Man is by nature a political animal."

Aristotle, 384-322 B.C.
Greek Philosopher

* And it's the animal part of politicians that

gives the rest of us a bad name.

~~~~~~

"When I was a boy I was told that anybody

could become President. I'm beginning to

believe it."

Clarence Darrow, 1857-1938
American Lawyer

* It's the benefits, stupid. No experience

necessary - lifetime pension."

~~~~~

"How can you govern a country which has 246

varieties of cheese?"

Charles de Gaulle, 1890-1970
French President

* Cheeseheads? I thought they were from

Wisconsin?"

~~~~~

"I'd rather be right than President."

Henry Clay, 1777-1852
American Politician

* Mom told me my stubbornness would keep

me out of the White House."

~~~~~

"Men's thoughts are such according to their

inclination, their discourse and speeches

according to their learning and infused

opinions."

Francis Bacon, 1561-1626
English Writer

* No, I don't believe Pat Robertson will ever

be President.

~~~~~

"No one is such a liar as the indignant man."

Friedrich W. Nietzsche,
1844-1900
German Philosopher

* Never mind pointing that finger, I still don't

believe you.

~~~~~

"In the early days of his power, he is full of

smiles, and he salutes every one whom he

meets."

Plato, 429-347 B.C.
Greek Philosopher

* Weren't you already warned to keep out of

Texas?

~~~~~~

"Get your facts first, and then you can distort

them as much as you please.

Samuel L. Clemens, 1835-
1910
American Writer (Mark Twain)

* I was giving liberty to journalists here, not

politicians.

~~~~~

"There cannot be a crisis next week. My

schedule is already full."

Henry Kissinger, 1923 –
American Statesman

* Good God! They broke into where?

~~~~~

"All politics, however, are based on the

indifference of the majority."

James Reston, 1909-?
Journalist

* Well, you voted for him, you live with it!

~~~~~

35

<u>Sports and Fair Play</u>

"All for one, one for all, that is our device."

Alexander Dumas, 1802-70
French Novelist
(The Three Musketeers)

* Just because three good friends wear lace on their shirts **doesn't mean they're not real men.**

~~~~~

"I am angry nearly every day of my life…but I

have learned not to show it; and I still hope to

learn not to feel it, though it may take me

another 40 years to do so."

Louisa May Alcott, 1832-88
American Novelist

* Miss Jones, send that memo to Mike Tyson.

~~~~~~

"From people who merely pray we must

become people who bless."

Friedrich W. Nietzsche,
1844-1900
German Philosopher

* And why the hell *should* God favor your

team to win over ours?

~~~~~

"Let me tell you the secret that has led me to

my goal. My strength lies solely in my

tenacity."

Louis Pasteur, 1822-95
French Chemist, Biologist

* Plus, I like to mix stuff together in the lab,

just to see if it will blow up.

~~~~~

"It could be worse. Suppose your errors were counted and published every day, like those of a baseball player."

Anonymous

* And you wonder why Pete Rose got ticked off? (I'm still not giving you my real name)

~~~~~

"He got a nick on his ear, and he quit."

Mike Tyson, (Still Living)
American Boxer

* I swear Your Honor, I don't hang out with

Ozzie Osborne anymore.

~~~~~

"Where there is neither love nor hatred in the

game, women's play is mediocre."

Friedrich W. Nietzsche,
1844-1900
German Philosopher

* I'm sorry. I said that before I played with

Navaratilova.

~~~~~

Epicurus Was Greek?

"Man is what he eats."

Ludwig Feuerbach, 1804-72
German Philosopher

*Remember, I said it first, not that eccentric

Tiny Tim."

~~~~~

"Ich bin ein Berliner."

John F. Kennedy, 1917-63
American President

* It's got strawberry jam in the middle? Sorry,

I was confused.

~~~~~

"Things they don't understand always cause a

sensation among the English."

Alfred De Musset, 1810-57
French Poet

* Mostly, it's good cuisine they don't

understand, which causes unpleasant

sensations in everyone else.

~~~~~

"Eating words has never given me

indigestion."

Winston Churchill, 1874-1965
British Prime Minister

* It was my wife's cooking that brought on that

foul – sorry, ladies **present.**

~~~~~

"You can tell the ideals of a nation by its

advertisements."

Norman Douglas, 1868-1952
Scottish Novelist

* What are these people eating that so many of

them suffer from irregularity?

~~~~~

<u>Art For Arts Sake</u>

"Art is a human activity having for its purpose

the transmission to others of the highest and

best feelings to which men have risen."

Count N. Tolstoi, 1828-1910
Russian Novelist

* Red squares amongst Blue Blobs! That just

makes me feel sick.

~~~~~

"Abstract art is a product of the untalented,

sold by the unprincipled to the utterly

bewildered."

Al Capp, 1907-79
American Cartoonist

* Please refer to Tolstoi. I'm feeling rather ill

right now myself."

~~~~~

"One picture is worth 10,000 words."

Frederick R. Barnard, 19?? -?
Writer

* And if you sell it to the tabloids it could be

worth the same in dollars.

~~~~~

"Scots, wha hae wi' Wallace bled,

Scots wham Bruce has aften led,

Welcome to your gory bed, Or to victory!"

Robert Burns, 1759-96
Scottish Poet

* Do ye nae think Mel Gibson looked silly in

that blue face paint?

~~~~~

"I cannot help it that my pictures do not sell.

Nevertheless, the time will come when people

will see that they are worth more than the price

of the paint."

Vincent Van Gogh, 1853-90
Dutch Artist

* You paid how many million? Damn. Makes

me wish I'd have taken better care of myself.

~~~~~

<u>Literate or Literature</u>

"The monuments of wit survive the

monuments of power."

Francis Bacon, 1561-1626
English Writer

* Personally, I think Ronald Reagan would

have made a great stand-up comic.

~~~~~

"I do not know any reading more easy, more

fascinating, more delightful, than a catalogue."

Anatole France, 1844-1924
French Novelist

* If you know what's good for you, you'll keep

your cotton pickin' fingers off my Victoria

Secret.

~~~~~

"I don't mind what language an opera is sung

in so long as it is a language I do not

understand."

Edward Appleton, 1892-1965
English Physicist

* Any chance of hiring a group of mimes?

~~~~~

"xxx dayes hath November, Aprill, Jvne and

September

Febrvary hath xxviii alone, And all the rest

have xxxi."

Richard Grafton, d.c. 1572
London Publisher

* If you haven't learned your Roman

Numerals, you can't play at the Coliseum!

~~~~~

"It is a good thing for an uneducated man to

read books of quotations."

Winston Churchill, 1874-1965
British Prime Minister

* I didn't mean this one.

~~~~~

"America is now given over to a damned mob

of scribbling women."

Nathaniel Hawthorne, 1804-
64
American Writer

* Thank goodness I'm dead, otherwise I'd

probably have to apologize for that statement.

~~~~~~

"So very difficult a matter is it to trace and find

out the truth of anything by history."

Plutarch, c.46-120 A.D.
Greek Philosopher

* I understand you've read Nixon's book.

~~~~~

"A classic is something that everybody wants

to have read and nobody wants to read."

Samuel L. Clemens, 1835-
1910
American Writer (Mark Twain)

* No, I can't say as I've ever read anything by

Danielle Steele.

~~~~~~

"Gars auld claes look amaist as weel's the

new."

Robert Burns, 1759-96
Scottish Poet

* After a quart of whiskey you couldn't write

intellibigably either.

~~~~~

"When thought becomes excessively painful,

action is the finest remedy."

Salman Rushdie, 1947 –
Indian/British Writer

* Had I made those verses rhyme perhaps I

wouldn't have had to go into hiding.

~~~~~

War and a Little Peace

"We shall fight on the beaches, we shall fight

on the landing grounds, we shall fight on the

fields and in the streets, we shall fight in the

hills; we shall never surrender."

Winston Churchill, 1874-1965
British Prime Minister

* Feel free to come on over here, you bastards,

'cause we're gonna kick your ass!

~~~~~

"You should never wear your best trousers

when you go out to fight for freedom and

truth."

Henrik Ibsen, 1828-1906
Norwegian Dramatist

* I told you I'd kick the crap out of you if you

came to the rally wearing those green plaid

pants.

~~~~~

"In the words of one of my more sympathetic

correspondents, it has turned out to be an

'annus horribilis.'"

Queen Elizabeth II, 1926 –
British Monarch

* Those damn kids, if they aren't aggravating

me with one thing, it's another.

~~~~~

"Whether you like it or not, history is on our

side. We will bury you."

Nikita Khrushchev, 1894-1971
President, USSR

* What fool was in charge of Chernobyl? I said

them, not us.

~~~~~

"I have fought against the people of the North

because I believe they were seeking to wrest

from the South its dearest rights."

Robert E. Lee, 1908-70
American General

* By 'North,' I didn't mean you Canadians.

Although, you did beat the dickens out of us

during that little skirmish in 1812.

~~~~~

"The Germans are like women, you can

scarcely even fathom their depths – they

haven't any."

Friedrich W. Nietzsche,
1844-1900
German Philosopher

* Of course, I'm German. I wouldn't dare say

that if I wasn't.

~~~~~

"It is humiliating to remain with our hands

folded while others write history.

It matters little who wins. To make a people

great it is necessary to send them to battle even

if you have to kick them in the pants. This is

what I shall **do.**"

Benito Mussolini, 1883-1945
Italian Dictator

* You shot me! I can't believe you shot me!

Oh no, not the rope too.

~~~~~

"The bullet that will kill me is not yet cast"

Napoleon Bonaparte, 1769-
1821
Emperor

* Aha, so they went for poison. How could I

have been so stupid?

~~~~~

"Mr. Wilkie, you know I grew up a Georgian

peasant. I am unschooled in pretty talk. All I

can say is I like you very much."

Joseph Stalin, 1879-1953
Soviet Dictator
(as said to Wendell Wilkie)

* No, I'm not light in the loafers, I just meant it

as a compliment

~~~~~

"War talk by men who have been in a war is

always interesting; whereas moon talk by a

poet who has not been in the moon is likely to

be dull."

Samuel L. Clemens, 1835-
1910
American Writer (Mark Twain)

* So you're Neil Armstrong – yes, I would like

to hear your story.

~~~~~

"A thick skin is a gift from God."

Konrad Adenauer, 1876-1967
German Chancellor

* Thank you. We Germans needed that.

~~~~~

It's Just Business

"The battle of competition is fought by

cheapening of commodities."

Karl Marx, 1818-83
Communist Manifesto

* I'm waiting for the end to these technology

wars before I upgrade my PC.

~~~~~

"Private information is practically the source

of every large modern fortune."

Oscar Wilde, 1854-1900
English/Irish Dramatist

* Show me a seller of address lists and I'll

show you a millionaire.

~~~~~

"Imprisoned in every fat man a thin one is

wildly signaling to be let out."

Cyril Connelly, 1903-74
English Writer

* I cannot explain Richard Simmons any fuller

than that.

~~~~~

"There's a sucker born every minute."

P.T. Barnum, 1810-91
American Showman

* I think that explains why someone would pay

$10.00 to see an Adam Sandler movie.

~~~~~

"If you can actually count your money, then

you are not really a rich man."

J. Paul Getty, 1892-1976
American Industrialist

* Don't try scaring me with that Ghost of

Christmas Past stuff. I'm rich and you're not,

so – nanny, nanny, nanny!

~~~~~

"I want the whole of Europe to have one

currency; it will make trading much easier."

Napoleon Bonaparte, 1769-
1821
Emperor

* How long does it take you people to catch

on?

~~~~~

Laurie James

"One finger in the throat and one in the rectum

makes a good diagnostician."

William Osler, 1849-1919
Canadian Physician

* I'm through for the day. Want to join me for

lunch?

~~~~~

"The most delicious of all privileges –

spending other people's money."

John Randolph, 1773-1833
American Politician

* Oh, to be in Washington, now that the

lobbyists are there.

~~~~~

"Entrepreneurship is the last refuge of the

trouble-making individual."

James K. Glassman, (1800-??)
Writer/Philosopher

* Mr. Gates, may I ask what non-English

speaking person you hired to create "Grammar

Check?"

~~~~~

<u>Articles of Faith</u>

"Religion is a great force – the only real

motive force in the world; but what you

fellows don't understand is that you must get a

man through his own religion and not through

yours."

George Bernard Shaw, 1856-
1950
English Novelist

* If it's those Watchtower people, I'm not

home.

~~~~~

"Dancing in all its forms cannot be excluded

from the curriculum of all noble education:

dancing with the feet, with ideas, with words,

and, need I add that one must also be able to

dance with the pen."

Friedrich W. Nietzsche,
1844-1900
German Philosopher

* What is it about dancing the Baptists just

can't understand?

~~~~~

"The reports of my death are greatly

exaggerated."

Samuel L. Clemens, 1835-
1910
American Writer (Mark Twain)

* Force me to visit one more European

cathedral claiming to house the body of St.

Peter, and it might kill me.

~~~~~~

"No people do so much harm as those who go

about doing good."

Mandell Creighton, 1843-1901
English Prelate

* OK, so Albert Schweitzer may have been an

exception.

~~~~~

"The Jews generally give value. They make

you pay; but they deliver the goods. In my

experience the men who want something for

nothing are invariably Christians."

George Bernard Shaw, 1856-
1950
English Novelist

* I've always thought it wise to beware of

television evangelists.

~~~~~~

"Avoid, as you would the plague, a clergyman

who is also a man of business."

St. Jerome, c. 342-420 A.D.
Christian Monk

* Believe me, George Bernard Shaw knew

what he was talking about.

~~~~~

"I look upon all the world as my parish."

John Wesley, 1703-91
Methodist Preacher

* And it's a big world - so my share of the

collections should be more than this!"

~~~~~

"If you really want to make a million – the quickest way is to start your own religion."

L. Ron Hubbard, 1911-1986
Founder of Scientology

* Sign up now – ask about our easy lifetime monthly payments."

~~~~~

<u>Law and Some Order</u>

"Vote for the man who promises the least, he'll

be the least disappointed."

Bernard Baruch, 1870-1965
Financier

* On second thought, now you've got to

consider the women too.

~~~~~

"Give me liberty or give me death."

Patrick Henry, 1736-99
American Statesman

* My mistake, I should have given you some

other options."

~~~~~

"A little rebellion now and then is a good

thing."

Thomas Jefferson, 1743-1826
American President

* I didn't mean for every damn President down

the road to take this literally.

~~~~~

"The malicious have a dark happiness."

Victor Hugo, 1802-85
French Novelist

* No wonder I couldn't get a job with the

tabloid publishers.

~~~~~

" The two oldest professions in the world –

ruined by amateurs."

Alexander Woollcott, 1887-
1943
American Writer

* Heidi Fleiss, meet F. Lee Bailey. F. Lee

Bailey, meet Heidi Fleiss.

~~~~~~

"A barristers' profession is such an uncertain

thing, especially if he won't undertake

unsavory cases."

Henrik Ibsen, 1828-1906
Norwegian Dramatist

* How was I to know that the Dream Team of

the late 20th century **would prove me wrong?**

~~~~~~

Sexual Revolution

"A compliment is something like a kiss

through a veil."

Victor Hugo, 1802-85
French Novelist

* What do you mean, you're charging me with

sexual harassment? I told you, it was a

compliment.

~~~~~

"Come live with me and be my love,

And we will all the pleasures prove…"

Christopher Marlowe,1564-93
English Dramatist

* Who said anything about marriage? I simply
said come and live with me, and yes; I know
your mother won't approve.

~~~~~

"Men seldom make passes

At girls who wear glasses."

Dorothy Parker, 1893-1967
American Humorist

* I said that before I understood how desperate

politicians could get.

~~~~~

"Be plain in dress, and sober in your diet;

In short, my deary, kiss me, and be quiet."

Lady Mary Wortley
Montagu, 1689-1762
English Writer

* Get out of those shorts, and from now on all I

want to hear is you screaming my name.

~~~~~

"Candy is dandy, but liquor is quicker."

Ogden Nash, 1902-71
American Humorist

* And if I were alive today I'd probably say

the same thing.

~~~~~

"Old men have need to touch sometimes with their lips the brow of a woman or the cheek of a child, that they may believe again in the freshness of life."

Maurice Maeterlinck, 1862-1949
Belgian Poet

* What do you mean, you're charging me with sexual harassment? It's a compliment!

~~~~~~

"All that we know who lie in gaol

Is that the wall is strong;

And that each day is like a year,

A year whose days are long."

Oscar Wilde, 1854-1900
English/Irish Dramatist

* Bugger! Bugger! Bugger!

~~~~~

"When the candles are out all women are fair."

Plutarch, c. 46-120 A.D.
Greek Philosopher

* And now that morning dawns – what the hell

was I thinking?

~~~~~~

"Whipping and abuse are like laudanum: you

have to double the dose as the sensibilities

decline."

Harriet Beecher Stowe,1811-
96
American Novelist

* I haven't been sniffing anything; I'm a

preacher's kid. I only know about those things

from hearsay.

~~~~~

"We are not amused."

Queen Victoria, 1819-1901
British Monarch

* Who said I have no sense of humor? I had an

affair with a hairy Scotsman, didn't I?

~~~~~

"And when you rise in the morning you will

find what I tell you is so."

Walt Whitman, 1819-92
American Poet

* Now, do you believe the old saying? Big

hands ......

~~~~~

"I married beneath me, all women do."

Nancy Astor, 1879-1964
American Socialite

* There's little to be said for a guy who asks

what kind of wine he should have with his

pancakes.

~~~~~

"Sexual intercourse is merely internal attrition

and the spasmodic excretion of mucus."

Marcus Aurelius, c. AD 161
Roman Emperor

* My apologies. I said that the morning I woke

up next to this ugly woman from Thebes.

~~~~~

"I have never yet seen anyone whose desire to

build up his moral power was as strong as

sexual desire."

Confucius, 551-479 B.C.
Chinese Philosopher

* I warned the Congressmen about that, but

would they listen."

~~~~~

" Mr. Watson, come here, I want you."

Alexander G. Bell, 1847-1922
Inventor

* Damn you, Watson, I didn't mean I wanted

you in *"that"* way.

~~~~~

"I came, I saw, I conquered."

Julius Caesar, 100-44 B.C.
Roman Emperor

* She looked a lot older than thirteen to me!

~~~~~

"Religion is by no means a proper subject of

conversation in a mixed company."

Lord Chesterfield, 1594-1771
British Politician, Writer

* You surprise me Madam, I didn't think you'd

be interested in strip poker."

~~~~~

"I am the love that dared not speak its name."

Lord Alfred Douglas, 1870-
1945
English Poet (Friend of Oscar Wilde)

* I'm giving you my rank and serial number,

and that's it, Your Honor."

~~~~~

"The only unnatural sex act is that which you

cannot perform."

Alfred Kinsey, 1894-1956
American Researcher

* Don't say I didn't warn you. Want me to call

the fire department?"

~~~~~

"Who loves not women, wine and song;

Remains a fool his whole life long."

Martin Luther, 1483-1546
German Theologian

* I consider myself a poet more than a

preacher. And you know how wild we artistic

types can get."

~~~~~

"The Duke returned from the wars today and

did pleasure me in his top-boots."

Sarah, Duchess of
Marlborough
1660-1744
English Duchess

* Dear Hugh Hefner: In response to your

request for photographs….

~~~~~

117

<u>Mental Gymnastics</u>

"Every man who has declared that some other

man is an ass or a scoundrel, gets angry when

the other man conclusively shows that the

assertion was erroneous."

Friedrich W. Nietzsche,
1844-1900
German Philosopher

* I'm sorry I called you a doofuss, but you did

look rather stupid in that Viagra commercial.

~~~~~

"The loveliest tune imaginable becomes vulgar

and insupportable as soon as the public begins

to hum it and the hurdy-gurdies make it their

own."

Joris Karl Huysman, 1848-
1907
French/Dutch Novelist

* If I hear "Raindrops Keep Falling on my

Head" one more time, I shall have to kill

someone.

~~~~~

"All our knowledge merely helps us to die a more painful death than the animals that know nothing. A day will come when science will turn upon its error and no longer hesitate to shorten our woes."

Maurice Maeterlinck, 1862-1949
Belgian Poet

* Don't you dare give my phone number to Dr. Kevorkian!

~~~~~

"No physician, in so far as he is a physician,

considers his own good in what he prescribes,

but the good of his patient; for the true

physician is also a ruler having the human

body as a subject, and is not a mere money

maker."

Plato, 429-347 B.C.
Greek Philosopher

* How was I to know there'd be such a thing as

HMO's?

~~~~~

"O Captain! My Captain! Our fearful trip is

done."

Walt Whitman, 1819-92
American Poet

* And thank you for not making me change

planes at Dallas/Ft. Worth.

~~~~~

"It takes two to make a marriage a success and

only one a failure."

Lord Samuel, 1870-1963
British Politician

* Ted Turner, Donald Trump, Woody Allen,

Newt Gingrich, et al. Please approach the

bench.

~~~~~

"The thought of suicide is a great consolation:

by means of it one gets successfully through

many a bad night."

Friedrich W. Nietzsche,
1844-1900
German Philosopher

* It's a joke, a joke! If you wrote the kind of

stuff I do, you'd have many a bad night, too.

~~~~~

"You read what Disraeli had to say. I don't

remember what he said. He said something.

He's no longer with us."

Robert Dole, 1923 –
American Politician

* What I need now is a pill that makes my

brain rise to the occasion."

~~~~~

"I have opinions of my own – strong opinions

– but I don't always agree with them."

George H. W. Bush, 1924 –
American President

* Apparently I need the same medication as

Bob.

~~~~~

"I just come to talk to the plants, really – very

important to talk to them, they respond I find."

Charles, Prince of Wales,
1948 –
Future King

* Try holding a conversation with some

members of my family and see how far you

get.

~~~~~

"I think, therefore I am."

Rene Descartes, 1596-1650
French Writer

* Stop that chattering in there. My brain is

starting to hurt.

~~~~~

"Playing 'Bop' is like Scrabble with all the

vowels missing."

Duke Ellington, 1899-1974
American Musician

* Y my nt ndrstnd t bt yll gt th drft."

~~~~~

"When a President does it, that means it's not

illegal."

Richard Nixon, 1913-94
American President

* That depends on what your definition of

"illegal" is.

~~~~~

"I suppose flattery hurts no one, that is, if he

doesn't inhale."

Adlai Stevenson, 1900-65
American Politician

* You don't understand, you can still get all

the same benefits without inhaling. Trust me.

~~~~~

<u>Philosophically Speaking</u>

"To err is human."

Victor Hugo, 1802-85
French Novelist

* So get off my back!

~~~~~

"Great blunders are often made, like large

ropes of a multitude of fibers."

Victor Hugo, 1802-85
French Novelist

* Do I have to explain everything twice?

~~~~~

"Canadians do not like heroes, and so they do

not have them.

George Woodcock, 1912-95
Canadian Writer

* Well, we have lumberjacks in plaid jackets,

and those guys in the red coats. You know, the

ones wearing the Smokey Bear hats.

~~~~~

"When I was young I found out that the big toe

always ended up making a hole in a sock. So, I

stopped wearing socks."

Albert Einstein, 1879-1955
Mathematician

* There is no truth to the rumor that I stopped

wearing pants for the same reason.

~~~~~

"Being an old maid is like death by drowning,

a really delightful sensation after you cease to

struggle."

Edna Ferber, 1804-72
American Novelist

* Whoa Tiger! Thanks for making me stop

struggling. Who knew?

~~~~~

"Those who have given themselves the most

concern about the happiness of peoples have

made their neighbors very miserable."

Anatole France, 1844-1924
French Novelist

* To you they're antiques; to me, they're a pile

of junk. Now get those old jalopies off my

front lawn!

~~~~~

Laurie James

"Home is heaven and orgies are vile

But I like an orgy, once in awhile."

Ogden Nash, 1902-71
American humorist

* Really, Larry Flint isn't such a bad guy once

you get to know him.

~~~~~

"Be nimble and light-footed, his father

encouraged him to run in the Olympic race.

"Yes," he said, "if there were any kings there

to run with me."

Plutarch, c. 460-120 A.D.
Greek Philosopher

* Did I mention I'd met George W.?

~~~~~

"Mathematics takes us into the region of

absolute necessity, to which not only the actual

world, but every possible world must

conform."

Bertrand Russell, 1872-1970
British Mathematician

* My apologies. I said that before some fool

invented new math.

~~~~~

"I never found the companion that was so

companionable as solitude."

Henry David Thoreau, 1817-62
American Writer

* So I died a virgin, is that so bad?

~~~~~

"The land of the faery – where nobody gets old

and godly and grave."

Wm. Butler Yeats, 1865-1939
Irish Poet

* Welcome to San Francisco. Please remain

seated until the aircraft comes to a full stop.

~~~~~

"A guy marries one sister. It doesn't work out,

and then years later, he winds up married to the

other sister."

Woody Allen, 1935 –
American Humor Writer (Hannah and
Her Sisters)

* Then again, it could be another relative

altogether.

~~~~~

Laurie James

"Truth never damages a cause that is just."

Mohandas K. Gandi, 1869-1948
Indian Statesman

* So I lied about my sex life – who doesn't?

~~~~~

144

"Famous remarks are seldom quoted

correctly."

Simeon Strunsky, 1879 - ?
Novelist

* I rest my case.

~~~~~

Quoted Author Page Numbers

Page Two

Page Three

ABOUT THE AUTHOR

Canada's first female comic strikes again! Laurie James, award winning speaker, performer, and comedy writer, offers her new book "What I Meant to Say Was" for a laugh a minute reading experience. She attributes her sometimes-bizarre sense of humor to having been born and raised in the cold wilderness of Canada, and with being a Baptist preacher's kid. Rather than performing her hilarious material, she now writes it. She currently lives in San Francisco in semi-retirement where she is writing her memoir, doing public speaking, and writing more funny stuff.

Printed in the United States
744100002B